DREAMWORKS

THE BOSS BABY

501 THINGS TO FIND

igloobooks

Introduction

Okay, Kid, listen up. I'm a busy baby with places to be and a nappy that's weighing me down, so I'll keep this brief. Business is business and if you want a head for business then you need to be sharp. This book will test your skills. Make it to the end and there's a corner office waiting for you.

"I say, you do. Got it?"

"B is for Boss. That's me, not you."

I run the show my way.

"These sales numbers are total poop!"

"You think being boss is easy." (Okay. It is easy.)

First, let's practise on the page opposite. Find the correct amount of each money type in the larger picture. When you've found them, you're ready to go!

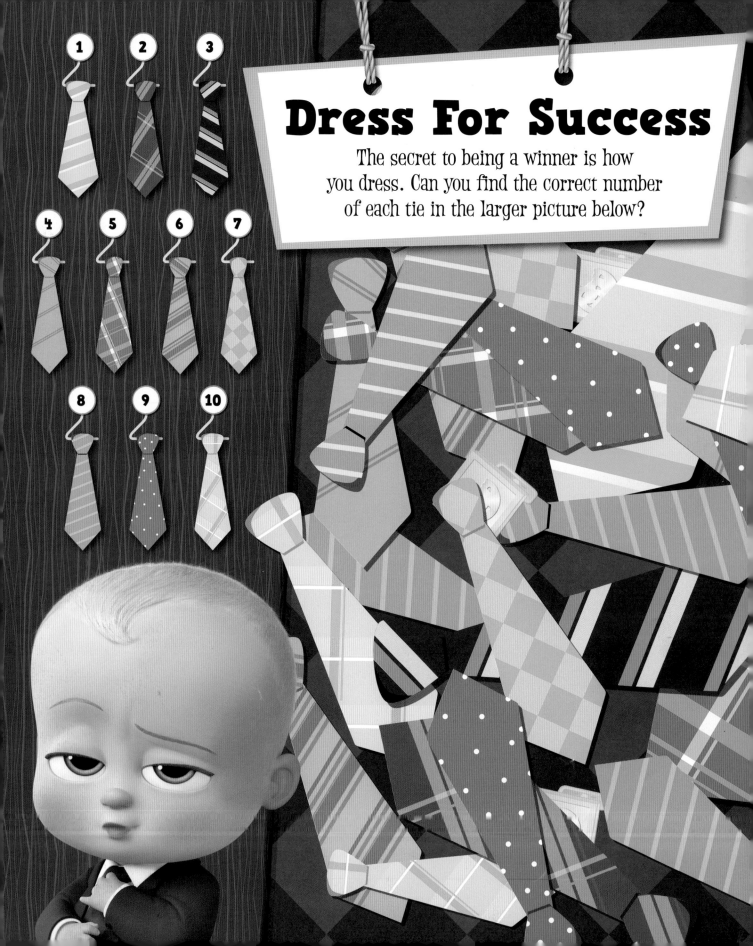

Dress For Success

The secret to being a winner is how you dress. Can you find the correct number of each tie in the larger picture below?

Pencil
Me In!

The pencil truly is mightier than the sword. Study this mess and find the right amount of each pencil in the scene.

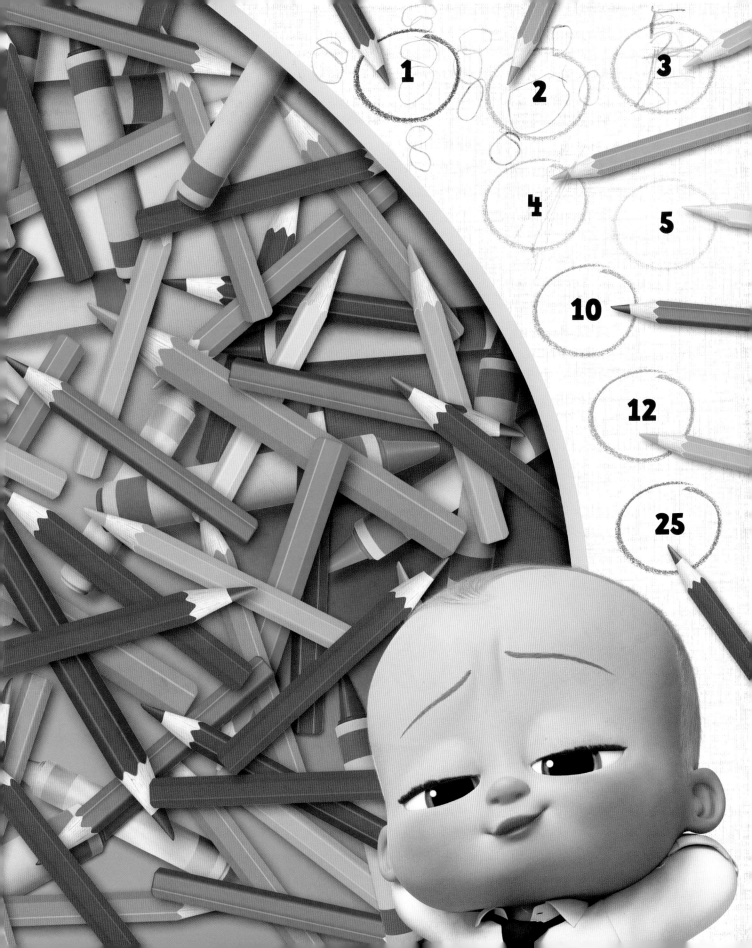

A Numbers Game

It's not all power naps and potty breaks, there's work involved too y'know. Find the correct amount of patterns hidden in the abacus below.

Business Is For Dummies

Even the best businessman needs his boo-boo once in a while. Can you find the right amount of each dummy in the larger scene below?

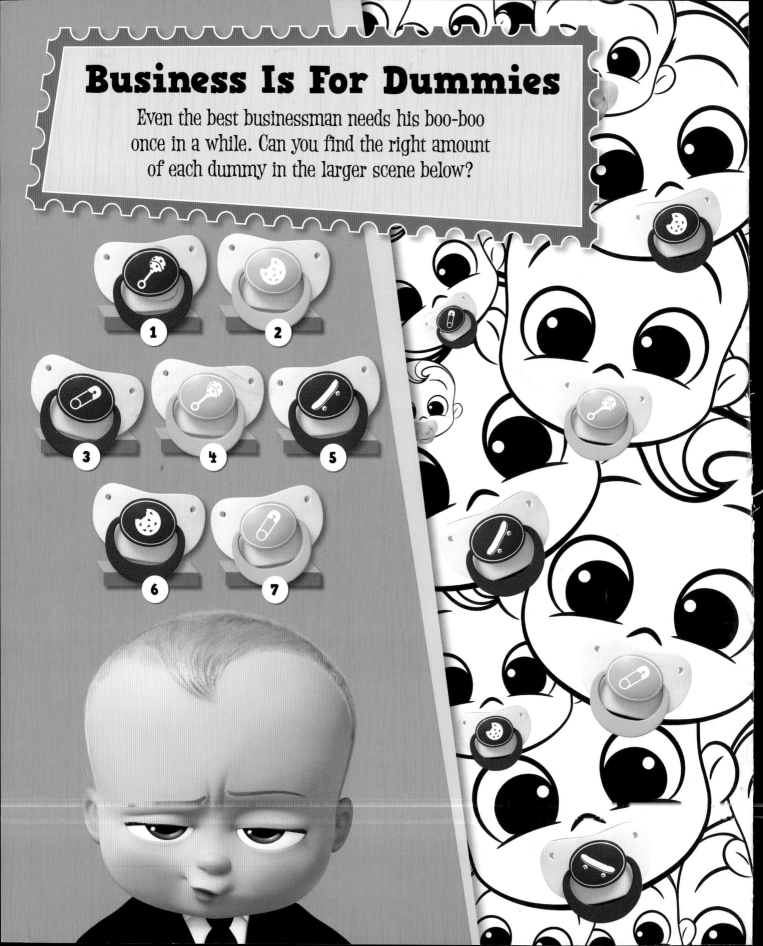

Call Me Boss!

A whole lot of me, what could possibly be better than that? Study the pictures closely and find the correct amount of each of my poses.

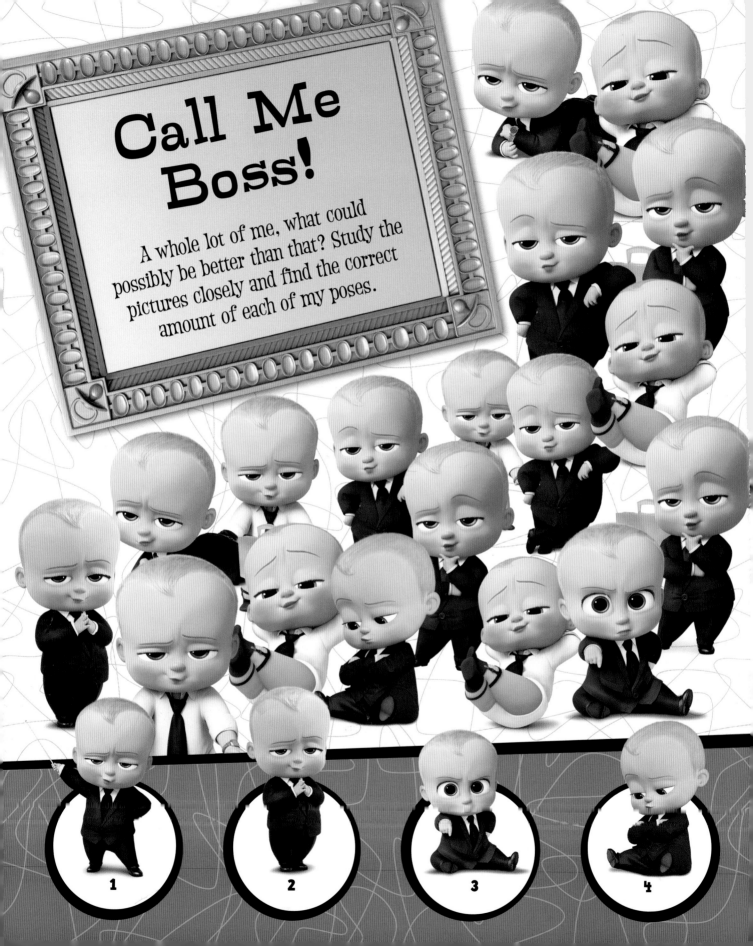

1

2

3

4

5

6

7

8

Playtime

Even in the world of business, everyone needs to take a break once in while. Can you find the correct amount of each block in the larger picture?

Cookies Are For Closers

The cookie – the greatest treat known to man and one that's only fit for the best babies. Study the picture and then find the correct amount of each cookie type.

1

2

3

4

5

6

Shake, Rattle and Roll

Business is about making yourself heard,
so grab a rattle and get shaking. Search the image
and find the correct amount of each rattle type.

1

2

3

4

5

6

7

8

It's Showtime

Become a success and everyone will know your name. Search the movie strips and find the correct amount of close-ups of each image.

1

2

3

4

5

6

7

8

9

10

Life's Golden

When you become a success, the world turns gold. Go back through the book and find each of these objects. Once you have, you'll be ready for that all-important corner office.

5 Gold Coins

5 Gold Dummies

5 Gold Rattles

5 Gold Balls

5 Gold Cufflinks

5 Gold Movie Boards

5 Gold Crayons

5 Gold Briefcases

5 Gold Cookies

5 Gold Blocks

There are two golden Wizzies hidden throughout this book. Can you find them?

**For more great
The Boss Baby books,
visit IglooBooks.com**

Giant Sticker & Activity

Okay, Kid, the world of business
is tough. If you want to get ahead,
then you need to stay sharp!

I've put together this book to keep you on your
toes so... ZZZ POWER NAP! Where was I? Oh, right,
complete the activities, decorate the pages and learn
all about my special mission. I've even added
over 1000 stickers for you, so get going,
but remember, cookies are for closers!

The Junior Novel

Life was great until HE arrived.
An annoying baby in a flashy suit.
Where did he come from? Why was he
here in MY house and, more importantly,
how could I get rid of him?

My name is Tim and this is my story
about the week I first met Boss Baby
and how he changed my life... forever.